洞月亮

CAVE MOON PRESS

YAKIMA 中 WASHINGTON

2019

On the Brink of the Sea

洞月亮
CAVE MOON PRESS
YAKIMA 中 WASHINGTON

Cover Art: *We Could Have Stayed Home* 25"x 19" (2011) by Eva Warrick
Book design by Doug Johnson

ISBN: 978-0-9797785-3-7

On the Brink of the Sea

Moná Toirésa Ó Loideáin Rochelle

On The Brink of the Sea

Poems

ACKNOWLEDGMENTS

Many thanks to the editors of the following journals in which poems in this collection first appeared, sometimes in different incarnations: *About Place Journal*, "My Confessor," "Song Weaver" (Fall 2013); *Grey Sparrow Journal*, "Constance (Winter 2016)," "One Thousand Days of Summer" (Summer 2017); *JAMA*, "Ariana" (June 2015); *Journal of Medical Humanities*, "Atonement" (previously "Lament for Liberia"), "Love in Darkness" (Autumn 2015); *Notre Dame Review*, "Cento: Laudato Si'," "Mallarmé Meets Valéry" (Autumn 2016); *Plainsongs*, "February" (Summer 2016); *Santa Fe Literary Review*, "Holy Terror" (2015); *The Antiginosh Review*, "Sand Hills," "Summer Light," "On the Brink of the Sea," "Sea Muse" (Spring 2016); *The Penwood Review*, "Our Lady of the Pines," "Litany of Birde," "Poet's Son" (Fall 2016); *The Southern Review*, "Barefoot Abandon" (Autumn 2016) and "Sacred Moment" (Summer 2016); *WA-129*, "Albariño" (December 2017). *Xavier Review*, "Into the Desert" (Spring 2015). "Nora's Child," "My Confessor" and "Song Weaver," appeared in *Mourning Dove* (Finishing Line Press, 2016).

I am indebted to the monks at Camaldoli Hermitage, Big Sur, California, whose generous grant provided the time to write in silence and solitude and to the *Fundación Valparaíso,* Mojácar, Spain, for an artist-in-residency grant. Thank you to Seattle University, whose talented faculty provided guidance.

Enormous gratitude and appreciation to Doug Johnson at Cave Moon Press who made this possible. I also thank John Pierce for his copyediting. Additional debts are owed to poets Kathleen Flenniken, Samuel Green, Jeffrey Levine, Anita Endrezze, and Holly J. Hughes for their sage advice; to readers Ann Nagle, Stella Rey, and Marilyn McLaughlin; and to my spiritual companions, Fathers Joseph, Paul, Peter, Ray and Brother Isaiah. Every poet needs to read and drink in good company, so *Sláinte* to The Old Boar and Earth & Vine on Bainbridge Island.

A special thanks to my husband, Joseph, and our children, Rachelle, and Jon.

Most importantly, my profound gratitude to *Doctors Without Borders/ Médecins Sans Frontières & Catholic Relief Services*, for bringing light into darkness. I support *Médecins Sans Frontières* and *Catholic Relief Services.*

For widows, orphans & refugees

Contents

IV

V

I

Cento: Laudato Si'

Before the world existed, the holy people made themselves visible by becoming the clouds, sun, moon, trees, water, thunder, rain, snow...that way, they said, we would never be alone. ~ LUCI TAPAHONSO

I

The poet's question
confronts the poem,
by way of the poem
the place, by way of
the place, the world.
Our world is gravely damaged.

Sister Earth cries.
What harm you've inflicted
on me through misuse and abuse
(acidification, rapidification, deforestation).

See how these words bend
under the weight of the wind,
word after word, end without end?
Listen to Brother Wind's gospel.
There is holiness on the earth.
I stand where beggars stand,
those dark and haggard ones,

drifting up and down. I grasp
you, and drifting like the wind
across the wild sea, I am still far away.

Sister Water weeps.
Why do you turn my wonderland
into underwater cemeteries?
I will show you light on a gull wing,
in a mussel shell glinting opal sunlight,
numberless shells on the shoreline,
on a shore of washed stones,
under a sky the color of stone
cloaked in mist.
Come to my ocean to harvest
sea kelp and pearls. Each rock pool
a garden of color, bronze and blue,
rose of coral algae, ochre of sponge,
where whelk and starfish turn
in the stillness of my garden.
Kneel before my white wall.
Write your name upon the water.
See the hours passing like clouds,
and then, lie as still as the clouds,
thinking of all that has been lost
in our lifetime, the sanctity of
water lost.

II

What of the wild fauna and flora
that children will never see,

lost forever? Sister Earth feeds
us in her sovereignty, producing fruits
with colored flowers and herbs,
blessing us with swift winged birds,
lions, stags, and leaping roes.

Dream chaste flowers, of being a dove
or a small cloud hanging above
a shredded moon. Will the small, white
dove return cooled by the breeze
of its flight and breathe the air?
Sink in the hems of your senses.
I hear your dreams like wind,
and willing like the trees
I speak to you many syllables.
I speak to you green meadows
coated bright with flowers.
I speak to you rivers glinting topaz.
You were made for love,
every leaf enleafing all
the grove of our eternal orchardists.

You're circling around God,
you've been circling for thousands of years.
Are you a falcon, a storm, or a vast song?
Whatever bird you used to be, hawk or tern,
fierce or shy, these birds are dead.
How have you contributed
to the disfigurement and destruction of creation?

III

Be forewarned of the impact
of degradation and war on the poor!
Hunger, famine, people eating anything
(lizards, barn swallows, salt grass).
Women wrapped in *lappas* waiting
on wood benches, their litanies washing
a blood moon. Or red clouds of smoke
and splinters of bone, skin sizzling,
one hundred and twenty ways they died alone.
Or was it together in front of the cross praying?
And then, the next day hummingbirds
took their hair from skulls to weave
nests under pear-shaped stars in
orchards of womblike fruit.
    I hear weeping.

IV

I hear desert waters
from a mountain stream,
the sound of hot springs
as they rise from the earth,
the sound of rain on desert stone.
Rest in the fragrance of sage.
Rest in the hummingbird's song.
Rest as a young child, again.
What of Brother Desert?
External deserts of our world

grow because our internal deserts
are wasted and vast!
We plunder her at will,
violence in our hearts,
reflected in sickness of soul,
soil, sea, and sky. In my visions, I see
    with winds and waters and woods.

V

Now, heed a poet's incantation:
    I am a wind on a jade lake
    I am a hawk above the cliff
    I am a tide that drags to death
    I am the hill I walk upon.
There is an island of serenity
in the poet's mind like June sun in an orchard,
a rustle in the silk of afternoon,
the droning of an ill-natured bee.
I wish to live free from hate
and make my verses, as rivers
moisten the earth, fresh and pure.

One Thousand Days of Summer

We were young and free as the sky was blue,
cliffs as high as heaven, skipping past buoys

bobbing a white-capped bay, and we spoke of
running away each day. My friend, fair

and homely, had one trillion nickels and a dime.
I, dark and comely, had one penny and a rhyme.

Life moved slowly in our towne by the sea
those thousand days of summer.

We careened and chanted that childhood song
Step on a crack, you'll break your mother's back!

I stomped each crack furiously. She leapt each
crack sheepishly—those thousand days

of summer by the sea, warbling like marsh
wrens on cat-o'-nine-tails joyfully.

Life moved slowly on that road by the sea—
those thousand days of summer by the sea.

We stole into our wee towne, stealing
penny candy in the shoppe by the sea,

skipping toward home happily, until
I trilled, 'Let's run away for eternity!'

Poor Deb wailed, 'No,' then ran home tearfully.
I scoffed, making my way to the salt marsh,

studying crabs burrowing in mudflats' gray.
By dusk fireflies burned bright. By twilight

the banshee screamed, 'Get your arse home,
you miserable piece of shite.' I balked,

'Screw you mum, you're a miserable gnome,' and
so it is with children unloved and thus this poem.

Holy Terror

'What would I give for a drink from the old well in Scituate,' Woodworth remarked to his wife Lydia. She replied, 'Put that in a poem.'
~ SAMUEL WOODWORTH

There was no possible way
I would stay in that day.
At eight in the morning
mum started: 'Go outside
and don't come home
'til supper.' Gone—
two miles of smiles,
cruising the elm-leafed
seaside street, weaving
helter-skelter on my
powder-blue Schwinn.
I'm beautiful (in cousin
Mary's a-bit-too-large,
hand-me-down shift).

Deb's waiting at her picture window
wearing her shite-eating grin—again—
dolled up in her fancy-schmancy
seer-sucker-pink pedal pushers.
I say, 'Come on, we're wasting the day.'
We beg fresh-baked Portuguese
sweet bread from Pitcock Farm,
pilfer June-bearing berries.
A three-mile strand

past beach plums,
past potato fields,
past Meeting House Lane,
past lichen-covered stone walls
and the old Scituate well
all leading to towne.

We lay our bikes on a white
clover meadow swarming
with 60,333 honeybees
(Deb resists all the way).
We tiptoe into the House of God
(Father Sullivan's off today),
with Jesus,
with Saints,
with the dead,

cleansing plum-stained
hands in the Connemarra
marble, gold-gilded font,
cross ourselves, incanting
'Protect us from all evil,'
like giggling seagulls.

Summer sun heats
empty pews through
blue-milk windows.
Deb's flip-flops
pitter-patter-clatter-clatter
off ghost-like emptiness.

'Shhh, take 'em off or I'll kill ya.'
An anarchist away from disarray,
I commandeer my musketeer—
'Let's rob Peter to pay Paul.'
'That's a sin!' she snivels.
'Eejit, quit your hullabaloo,
or I'll gobsmack you.'

We poach pennies,
nickels, dimes too, lost
treasures under kneelers,
offering coins and prayers
to Jesus, Mary, Joseph.
Light seven votive candles
for our dreams,
for the dead,
for my dad.

My mood shifts
when we walk
toward Second Cliff—
NO JUMPING OFF BRIDGE.

'I won't do it,' Deb wails.
't's high-tide. I scale the rail
and swan dive.

I'm just this side of heaven.
It's only noon, and
I'm alive.

Mallarmé Meets Valéry

What does one do to undo lies untrue?
Would a child so young and in disarray
turn and walk the road anew?

Acts of violence never misconstrue!
She dreamed blissful dreams with *Mallarmé*—
but what would she do to undo lies untrue?

Place her right shoe on her left askew?
Listen to ocean waters say, *come away*,
then turn and walk the road anew?

Cease the superficiality. Who
defiles a child of four anyway?
What does one do to undo lies untrue?

She fought his violence, it's quite true,
fighting his stench and perversity too. Pray
she turns and walks the road anew.

In a drift of books, albeit few,
she escaped to *Ambroise Valéry.*
What does one do to undo lies untrue?
Turn and write the road anew. *Adieu.*

Sand Hills

They dwelt on sand hills by the shore south of Boston,
living off the catch of the sea—cod from the ocean,
clams in mudflats, storm-tossed moss on the strand.

They ate carrageenan pudding, fasting each Friday on brackish
clam broth—they thought themselves blessed by no debt, for the sea
roared to the east and the sun set to the west.

Days were full of storms and floods, gales and granite, breakers
and hail, for the Atlantic was a fickle friend; they mistrusted summer
folk, blue bloods, and purebred dogs; they did not covet Cadillacs

or envy yacht-club fools, for storms kept them anchored,
floods made them meek, waves swept them low. They understood evil,
tossing salt on the floor and holy water under the door—

Jesus, Mary, and Joseph. Their children were whooping cranes,
rebels on a rampage, mayhem at Mass, no sailor's delight.
Their mums would shout, *Get outta my sight you miserable shites!*

for they were morons, cretins indeed. Heedless, they scaled
seawalls, dove free fall into the sea by their shabby
makeshift shanties. They lived before texting, Twin Towers,

political correctness. And there's *mindlessness* meditation,
ISIS, Vilazadone, the euro and Yamoussoukro. They told tales
of sea hags and shipwrecks in icy cold waters but never spoke

ill of the dead nor suffered fools lightly. Trust was a must
amongst squalls and the mystery of God. They were storytellers
who were forever sinning and gutting shoal-water cod.

Laud the immigrant, *na hÉireannaigh*, for they worked the coast
with Acadians, traded fish for sweet summer corn with Cape Verdeans,
eschewing the country club crowd. Their joy

was weak tea with sugar, a red sky at night, a skunk on the run,
April Fool's Day, a potful of lobster, and the full moon dancing
on a flood hightide. They were bright whitecaps laughing,

a summer breeze, basking seals in the autumn sun. Their town
was not the city but a place where Father Sullivan baptized
their babies and buried their dead. They walked on water,
they walked the jetty off Jericho Road, moods buoyant as dories
in the harbour moored for the night. It was good to stand
on the shore, watch the ebb and flow of the tides, and it was good

to watch the hyacinth sea crewl to a fine cerulean blue.

The Girl and the Bob-o'-link

My brother made me angry,
my mum made me sad—
I'd only asked one question,
their answer made me mad!

So on that sunny May Day,
I did a childlike thing—
I climbed out of my window
and ran away that spring.

I found a path with trees and birds,
and a singing Bob-o'-link.
He asked, 'Where are you going?'
then gave a silly wink.

'Climb up my willow
and hide within my tree,
I have a broken wing,
but I can set you free!'

And then the Bob-o'-link called out,
'Why did you run away?'
'They said that I'm fatherless!'
'O dear! Don't fear he's not so far away.

I've heard your father lately
in the rustling of the trees,
he's writing on the wings of birds,
and on the summer breeze.

You're his black-eyed Susan,
his lovely daffodil,
don't loathe your mum and brother,
for love is just God's will.

Love the clouds, the passing clouds,
love the bird's wing-beat,
love the summer's ocean wind,
love is bittersweet.'

Summer Light

I am a willow of the wilderness loving the wind that bends me.
~ R. W. EMERSON

Play with me in the willow tree.

I prefer to stay home and not be in your willow tree.

Come with me to the lime-green willow tree   we'll climb
to the highest boughs and hide in the weeping willow tree.

Be with me while the willow tree sways.

We'll swing on willow branches this summer day
recite *Mallarmé*   dance in pleasing light

daydream   weaving wedding bouquets.

I will not come to your willow tree   for my mother
weeps and frets with fear when I stray away from home.

I am home.   Here sea winds strum golden strings
of my willow tree. I am in the good company of dragonflies

their wings   afire   faceted amethyst and sapphire
as dragonflies darn and mend the whispering willow tree.

Let's hide until night   loving summer light   ciphering
secrets on the amber bark of my green weeping willow tree.

Nora's Child

I

Once there was a child in the Isle of Eire whose name was Mary. That child was sweet and pure with rosebud lips. Born into the ancient clan of *O'Ceileachair*, meaning *lover of company*, born into the ancient line of kings, *Mac Cárthaigh*, meaning *loving*, born between Éamon de Valera and Joyce. Mary was much loved. When Mary was three years of age, unrest and famine blighted her holy home under the crushing hands of unholy hegemony. Which is when, placed into the hands of a friend, Mary boarded the SS CATALONIA bound to America. Three weeks, three days, three hundred seventeen in steerage, three dead.

II

Boston Precinct 3 proved prosperous for the *Paddies*. Mary most lovely stole the heart of Thomas *O Loideán*, meaning *from the linden tree hill*. They dwelt by the sea where the tides collide—blessed with seven children named for saints: Marie, Elizabeth, Irene, Louise, Francis, Christopher, and James. One day at daybreak the sun set red in the west. Countless gannets *kok kok koked* on the cliffs. Word came that Thomas's ship went down at sea. This is a poem of sadness.

III

Sadness is sadness, although we like to call it other things. Violent sadness sent Mary to insanity. She never came back. The Fourteenth Census of the United States, in crisp cursive columns, told the story: five children placed in industrial school; the two babies placed in an aunt's care; Mary, the mother, assigned as an *inmate* of the state.

IV

Exiled to the farm colony for fifty years in the company of eighteen-hundred half-wits, melancholiacs, maniacs; imprisoned in perpetuity—to unpaid labor—Mary knit. In her sadness, in the brick wards set on the hills of the Hassanamisco Tribe, the land of pitch pine and shrub plain, Mary did as she was told. At night—much deranged Thelonious Monk—howled madly haunting Grafton's halls. I only meant to learn what no one ever spoke of. Not this, never this.

V

If I'd met her—I want to believe my grandmother and I would knit worsted wool woven in our clan's design, and walk toward the whorling seas, holding hands, enchanted.

Aunt Louise

Consider the hand you're dealt. My father,
James, was a poet, my mother the daughter
of a lobsterman. My grandmother, grandfather,
and father died the same year. I was one—
my mum was twenty-one. I think about those
early years, when my aunt pressed books into my hands—
Treasury of Irish Myths and *Children of Lir.*
And I'd press them over my heart in awe and gratitude.
We walked once on a June day, touching sweet
honeysuckle stamens to our tongues, watching
cloudscapes—a prince on a galloping stallion fleeing
Spanish galleons. Making our way toward
Third Cliff, I'd not confide my secret. I now
know she knew. A rebel, I'd hide in the lilac grove
for hours, run away to the cliffs. Disobey, disobey,
disobey. My mum, fierce with wrath, beat me—
leather belt, metal hanger, bloody flyswatter,
even the soup ladle—many, many times. But
never, never did she strike my face. I've wondered
why I'd laugh in defiance when I wanted
to cry. For years it was that way,
my aunt riding the train from Mattapan,
gifting a hardcover book filled with hope.
Whisperings of who I'd become?
Someone I thought I'd never be?
A secret keeper?

I Told My Children the Secret

Strange how I still remember the acrid stench of
low tide by my aunt's shanty on a summer day. I
was five. Because of the boys, my mum left me
outside while she and my aunt got drunk.
I think a lot about that day. I was content
to watch the cloudscape blow in from the sea. I
heard the slightest unseen stirring, a whispering
from the reeds of the marsh. And then I saw the
turtle—safe—under a piece of driftwood. So
much I still don't understand. I stoood
in the marsh for half an hour holding
the box turtle, imagining she was my best friend.
My cousin—quite drunk—approached us,
grabbing my body, snatching my turtle.
Do you remember that I was five?
Smattered blood, patterned shell, fell
onto the narrow beach path.
I won't leave out the worst.
The reprobate raped me. I've tried
to forget. If only I could forget.
If only I could re-create
that day. I should tell you
that I've told my children about him—
the unspeakable rending
of innocence.

II

From the Words of Conor Kenny, 2017

Dusk descends. Like storm petrels in flight, passengers cry out for the dead. Dawn ascends. In a boat adrift, a woman weeps. Her brother's tomb—sighs like a mother. The sea is blue. The sea is clear.

Famine

for Alfred Davies

And they hung the infants from their mother's necks.
1 MACCABEES 1:61

'How bad are things down there?'
'What the hell, we don't know.
Words can't describe it.' And there,
annealed in fire as craven hunger
hungers, an image, a child
that is, that was, that is to come
is captured in a journalist's lens.
Mothers' lips gasp apocalypse,
as icon after icon after icon—
Facebook, Twitter, Instagram—
image children as caverned tombs.
Sixteen million children the size
of fledgling birds lay wasting.
        When did I see you hungry?
A crucible of love traverses eleven kilometers
to a camp, her infant entwined—a dying vine.
And Alfred, an aid worker, places sugar
water on the tongue of Fana, six months old
(more or less), three kilograms (more or less);
and Adama, her mother, fifteen years old (more or less),
washes Fana, swaddling her in cotton. A thin
man places Fana in a wheelbarrow, carting
her to the burial place. And Alfred

says, ‘Lack of food’s a disaster, but
every time I think I know how bad it is,
we find it’s worse, we find
children cut in half.’

Miraculous Water Birth of Jésus

I want the word
of women's plight,
word upon word,
poem upon poem,
pronounced.
August warms
Libya's coast, winds blowing
off the Mediterranean Sea.
Fawn-eyed women mewl
in pain—prison walls echoing.
Guards' guns sodomize.
Women bleed rivulets.
One escapes. And in a boat
on lemon water, sun-blessed
dolphins breach
as life throbs in her
refugeed womb.
No midwife hands.
Burning sun, brine-soaked
lips. Wracked,
weary, worn. And then,
the sea went mute,
as the child was born.
The mother wakes to rescuers:
A Senegalese man I didn't know
held my hand and wrapped my baby
in a scarf. I named him Jésus.
These words sound like a miracle,
like Jesus walking on water.

Atonement

I

Make room for delays, for donated secondhand rags
enjambed into crammed bag—
        Michael Kors, Façonnable, Dolce, and Gabbana.
Make room for mind-bending Liberia.

Halfway. We meet outside Heathrow's House Haven Pub over greasy
cod, malted chips, ruby stout. Boarding for Amsterdam. Mum's parting
wisecrack comes to mind—sipping Seagrams and Sprite, sucking a
Virginia Slim Menthol Ultra-Light, slurring—
        'You're soft as shite.'

We slam the tarmac, dodging fighter planes and ack-acks.
Monrovia's a cacophony of chaos, a sultry abaddon as adust

bodies sway, skinny hawkers stealing bubble-wrapped suitcases.
We wait. We wilt like Madonna lilies in August. In high spirits,
Sister Barb, companion to Saint Francis, a tour de force,

roars to our rescue—welcoming us to the land of doped-upped soldiers,
three civil wars, two million refugees, three hundred
fifty thousand dead. Yet, Barb never fled. We speed past
Médecins Sans Frontière mud-spattered jeeps, scattered tanks,
shattered schools, reading postwar billboards.

Gauguin daubed masterpieces in vermilion, viridian, violet—
        Stop Rape
        Love your mother

Stop Beating Women
Women's Bodies Are NOT Battle Grounds

Soberly, we pass rubbled JFK, aka 'Just for Killing', hospital. In
waking stupefaction, we seek quinine, Tanqueray, a torpor of
lime must prevent malaria downtime.

II

We work Mother Teresa's House of AIDs. Cachectic, swollen-bellied
orphans amongst scents of cleanliness. Diaper-clad babies waul, crawl
to and fro on holy ground, kissing our lips like nipping pups. Nuns
in blue-white saris cleanse crusted sores with Ivory, feed famished
infants Nestlé, scrub stained linoleum with Lysol as they cheerfully sip
Coca-Cola.
Blessed are the clean of heart.

III

West Point's slum crowns the coast with feces-filled
streets. More billboards adorn bombed walls. Mary Cassatt's
mothers and babies in chartreuse, rose, royal blue—
Please Don't Make Me an Orphan
Rape, Rape, Rape, Seek Free Treatment

Riffraff beat and rock our jeep, lobbing stones as
Barb weaves labyrinth streets to Star of the Sea, a
refuge for refugees. Ward after ward—cholera,
sleeping sickness, HIV. No running water, no
electricity, no drugs.

Out of the darkness,
a blind boy, a crippled boy, a boy called
Momolu climbs my body like a mona
monkey, kissing my tears like a thirsty storm
petrel. Momulu brailles my face for
friendliness.
        He smells of bedstraw.

IV

I study numbers. Nearly 90 percent
of 'women' raped, eight-five-percent know
perpetrator, most under eighteen, of these, half are
under twelve, of these, one in ten are under four.
Women wrapped in *lappas* sway on wood benches
in the church on the hill, sharing litanies of
violence. Five-, fifteen-, fifty-year-olds, washing
us in blood. Canticles of sorrow.
Blessed are they who hunger for righteousness.

Make room in your heart. Hear their words.
        Blessed are those who mourn.

        'I remember six hundred and sixty-six child soldiers.
        I remember names—*Walking-Fucking, Frisky-Rebel,*
        Domination. I remember my twelve-year-old grandson
        high on khat, tracking me down like a lioness,
        casting me down on unholy ground,
        his *friends* raping me over and over again.
        My blood painted the flowers.'

'I'm nine. I'm an outcast.
Thirteen "freedom fighters" took us from the
fields. Some high. Some drunk.
I cried for my mother under the shadow
of the cacao tree. Like wild pigs, they
trampled me, leaving me for dead under
the shade of a fragrant lime tree. When I
awoke, ten thousand swordtail butterflies
had clothed my naked body.'

'They came in the night. Vile vipers
stripped us: sodomites, feral beasts
of night despoiled my daughter.
She was four. I was fourteen.
I can't forget. I can't forgive.'

We sit with ghosts of Gehenna at a blue wall of sorrow.
How long will it be, holy GOD, before you sit in judgment
and avenge our blood on the inhabitants of the earth?

V

To escape landscapes of misease,
Barb and I go to Mamba Point. And there,
in luxury, journalists order *Château Angélus,*
waxing eloquent overtures of war (we drink
Guinness). An oleander moon illumes
the Atlantic. By midnight the fuel's gone,
lights die. 'Barb, why in God's name do you
stay in this place?' 'Atonement.'

VI

On a brilliant dawn fragrant with tuberose,
I awake in the convent to screams
echoing off bullet-blasted, barbed-wired
walls imbedded with glass shards. Ah, it's
only the schoolgirls! Angels of light, birds
of the soul, open my heart.

VII

One lone moan groans within immaculate
whitewashed walls. Nine months, nine days, nine
hours, nine minutes molded in her mother's
womb. The midwife's calm. The father clepes
for a son.

Covered in a crimson caul a daughter's born.
Her mother sings—
Banuwa, banuwa, banuwayo,
Ananoneniolano,
Ananoneniolano.

They name her Ariana, meaning *most holy*,
as they believed all would be well.

I can't shake her name.

Ariana

Sweat wets Ariana's hair,
sculpting sable curls
into a crown of black opals.

Ariana appeared like an atrate
angel, swaddled in a pale
lappa at our door.

In the morning she is half here
like a black swallowtail, nearly
extinct and rarely seen.

At noon, the white sheet,
once fragrant with bleach,
turns speckled red.

By evening, she lingers with moonless
eyes. I can no longer breathe
in my masque of mourning.

Then night comes,
and Ariana, small as a doll,
is gone.

Virologists tell us that 5 species
of Ebola were born 40 years ago,
near the *Legbala* River. There—
Sudan and the Congo
buried their dead.

What can I write about a child who dies?

MSF Monrovia Midnight 9th of September
Ariana 12 months old cause of death Ebola
no surviving family. *Charles de Foucauld MD*

Adonai and the Mai Aini Refugee Camp, 2017

Imagine mornings being as long as boswellia blooming—wild figs,
roasting green coffee, soldiers conscripting we children at play

as we hide in the marketplace—and evenings a soft blue-gold,
praying bead after bead, in a white room cooled by the sea—

songs of my mother comforting me. I want wings. I want
to be the wind. I flee with my three Tigrinyan friends.

Avoiding Afar caravans, we walk with wild goats
in the dark, past carcasses of camels strewn on dunes.

One night when the moon was at its thinnest, desert
jackals tracked us, pressing AK-47s to our heads.

In an unspeakable mêlée, the jackals laughed *She's only
an Eritrean.* By morning the trade winds covered her.

We arrive at Mai Aini. They give us bread, sandals,
a bed. What will I do? What does it matter?

And in the mud church, I watch a Jesuit pray
bead after bead, pressing his hand against

his heart, as if holding an injured mosque
swallow. And on the altar frankincense burns,

and in the incense, I see my family
in the white room—without me.

Constance

simple in the sense
she sang in Kiswahili
and thought all was well
and invisible in the sense
she spent days on her knees
washing floors with an upside-down
trash-can lid filled with filthy water
she glanced askance at burka-clad
whores walking through HIV
clinic doors   nevertheless
she had fire-souled grace

bound since birth
to seven days of work
to earn seventy shillings
to feed her seventeen children
to keep her home
in the slums of Mombasa
she scrubbed floors
with strong hands
her body sour
with sweat

each noon
she'd whisper
Yesu Kristo
as an imam
wailed *Mawlānā*

hers was a world I didn't understand
she was a fresh breeze in a sweltering room
she was a mother scorned by others
she was a song that nobody knew
she was a saint among sinners
she was a friend seldom found

I've missed her since the day I left

Copts of Egypt

Christians flee from villages like the Jews before them,
sorrowful. Hatred was, is, will be. Blood and debris.

And the children? In the rubble?

A tent tattered blue. A woman, cold as a stone,
weeps in her cot. Love turned sorrowful.

And the children? In the rubble?

In the monastery pilgrims pray, 'Lord forgive them.'
Icons of malachite and verdigris watch sorrowfully.

And the children? In the rubble.

Love in Darkness

It is difficult to get news from poems, yet men die miserably every day for lack of what is found there. ~ WILLIAM CARLOS WILLIAMS

I

Boarding a battered Belarusian Bombardier, I see tattered
satchels on torn seats nest like albatross on a cliff's ledge
as chickens cackle. I listen to the febrile trill of a little child.
Seven guards hold seven AKMs to the throat of a shackled
    suzerain. I listen to guttural Soviet commands.

Traversing the Steppes on the banks of the Kura,
Kolkhida Lowlands greet beaches of the Black Sea—
and there barbed-wire binds the border crossing, in fear,
we argue with the guards, watching us suspiciously,
the shadows of war incomprehensible on the road to Sukhum.
    Appalled, I throw up.

Plague: infectious disease spreading rapidly with death rates.
Multidrug resistant tuberculosis: resistant to most powerful drugs,
affects lungs, brain, kidneys, spine, floats in air several hours,
spreads through coughing, sneezing, speaking, singing.
Épidémiologiste: One who studies epidemic 'dis-eases.'

I'm a spook, a closer, I study dog-eared data.
The fieldco shows me my 'office,' a heaterless closet.
My mind tumbles like absinthe in a labyrinth as I listen
to one-hundred and forty-four-proof Abkhazian double-talk.
    What's bullshit, what's not?

Long days spent visiting missions and squalor in the sobriety
frozen cisterns—Selaphiel the Turk translates for us: Gabriela
the nurse, Rafal the log, Uriel the doc, Barachiel the tech from Liberia,
and *moi*, the American *épidémiologiste*, frantic with worry.

On the hard crust of snowdrifts we drive threading roads,
and rapt in concentration we grow quiet, too full of fear to talk.
Full of fear. Work: the outpost's remote. Work: rows of beds,
they're wasting away. Work: Nino was just a child lying in the bed
(accompanied by the translator), just a child. I'm ambushed.

She reminds me of my daughter. Slowly she speaks—
'Everyone's dead, my mother, brother, sister. I take
thirty pills a day. Have pity on me, end these miseries.
I want to play in the salty sea.' TB, dragon slayer of children.

II

Sunday, we stroll streets of streaming sewage, abandoned
buildings, deserted homes. Mothers mourn sons, sons
shot point-blank. Grief. Corpses left twelve deep. Grief.
We're told three hundred thousand refugees fled. We watch
lonely old men in black, moth-eaten wool drink black-market
vodka, playing backgammon on alder boards.

Putin unplugged the power grid yesterday;
he did today, as he will tomorrow. Minutes, hours,
days without water, without heat, without light.
It's Christmas. Cloistered in the compound,

we ignite beeswax candles, sup on *khachapuri*,
down *Putinka* in prisms of fire, huddling children
terrorized in the dark. I've never been one for long
nights, and retreat to my four-by-six cell, and
like a monk, I pray—
    Jesus Christ, Son of God, have mercy on me a sinner.
    Jesus Christ, Son of God, have mercy on me…
    Jesus Christ, Son of God, have mercy…

I'm snow drifting, dreaming all is calm in America.

III

It's midnight in Zugdidi, mission post
on the east hills of Georgia. I'm fractured
like the cracked glass in the room.
I write my name on the frost

to remember who I am. The cook calls
'*Bonjour. De quoi avez-vous besoin?*'
'*Je ne parle pas bien français.*'
She shrugs 'Do you want *café*?'
Merde, I hope Rosetta Stone refunds the 300 euro.

A new team arrives—gypsies
from Marseilles, Bordeaux, Kinshasa,
Monrovia, Port Townsend. Lion-hearted
Argonauts they traveled permafrost hills hidden
between then and now at minus
11.1111 degrees Celsius.

The military-green *hôpital's* cinder-block walls
hold holy icons, smell of camphor, soap, and
candlewax. Cell after cell, convalescents fast
like hermits, kissing Saint George—slayer
of dragons, aura of light, protector of the poor.

The scent of sorrow lingers in each room:
a child, a woman, an old man suffer
twenty thousand pills, two hundred
injections, two years of psychosis,
deafness, pain in solitary confinement.

It's New Year's. *Gauloises* gold with flame
anesthetize the pain. We drink rivers of wine,
bodies swaying side by side in pixilating light,
every Georgians' a poem.
I need to leave this place.
I need to go home.

Field Notes

Mission: No sleep in a cheap seat on an economic,
near-comic flight. Traveling light, my worn
knapsack brings back memories of laughter
in good company. But by the third
connection, usually Amsterdam,
        a restlessness of place—
be it Ukraine, Iraq, Afghanistan—
        troubles me.

Wonder: What's with this mutilated
world where word and war close borders?

Assignment: Arriving amidst hawkers
and psyops I ask the driver (albeit politely)—
Where are we, a war zone? He laughs politely—
Bienvenue en République Démocratique du Congo,
        our land of no roads.

Compound: Armed men guard makeshift wards.
And here I am, as if I'd always belonged,
working—smelling thunderstorms,
cholera, measles, trypanosomiasis—
in fluttering, curtained malaria tents.
        A child wades
rivers, skirts shit-faced *soldiers* stoned
on banana liqueur, her child entombed.
I ask—
        How long have you laboured?

Note: 12-year-old presents in prolonged
labour. Stillbirth @ 0130. ⊠, 2 kilos,
Apgars 0-0. Maternal death @ 0230.
Cause–Total abruption.
Thérèsa Ramón Hernández, CNM

Home: Sage-painted mesas
of the Sangre de Cristo's turn violet—
burning piñon shifts my mood.
Mother, midwife, wife within
adobe walls, cotton curtains fluttering.
    I can't sleep.

Tell me how to cure myself when sorrow weeps.

III

Recension

We're told our faces rhyme. She divides me. Why did I react so strongly? She didn't hold me or kiss me or say the word—*love*—until she died. Hatred has its limits. I've spent too much time in moldy wrath. I've become someone I do not like. I look at her now, she's so old. How could I have been so filled with hate? Quiet gray fills the room. She's afraid. I put my arms around her. She tells me, *I love you*. She's gone and I'm alone. My mother's death unearths my sins.

The Girl and the Jade-Eyed Hawk

Once upon a time there was a family with vast wealth
who dwelt in the faraway Land of Enchantment. One day,
a cold north wind howled and growled as a stealth
plague pounded their adobe walls. In great dismay,
the father lay dying and cried, 'Daughter dear, pray
each day, trust in the LORD always, and may
love endure forever.' Then the sun and moon
darkened. An owl yowled an omen of misfortune.

Heartless and greedy, the brother and mother
cast the sweet young girl away. Saddened, Isabel
sought solace in the Jemez wilderness. No other
maiden was purer—a mestizo, a *mirabelle*,
a *bois brûlé*. O, what did the owl foretell?
She lived amongst creatures of the wilderness—
owls, wolves, quail—free from bitterness.

Each night she slept on the floor by the door
as the stream sang a joyful melody,
as the nightingale (whom she adored)
sang in the weeping willow merrily.
One lone hawk's shadow lit quietly
upon her each dawn. He left moon pearls,
and silken spider webs with spindles and whorls.

Storytellers spun tales of Isabel's kindness
and purity. But over time, word reached
both mother and brother! Hating her meekness,

cursing her with wickedness, they beseeched
a serpent to snipe her each day. She screeched,
but, he paid no heed, poisoning day after day.
She wept, he crept—Oh, he would not go away.

Five years passed—a crow cawed, 'I know how
to break your curse. Climb the mesa's twelve steppes.'
She did—to no avail. From the silver willow bough,
a desert jackal howled, 'Forbear without misstep,
fast for forty days.' Despite no misstep—
she failed! (Yes, this tale sounds quite absurd.)
But when she finally prayed her father's words

a villanelle of roses fell,
the stream's joy sang forth.
Swooping down the jade-eyed hawk killed
the snake as a rainbow broke forth,
and suddenly all grew quiet. Thenceforth,
encircled by heaven's turquoise lovescape,
Isabel enjoyed the amethyst cloudscapes.

Isabel danced a tripudiant stream,
Isabel sang a nightingale celeste,
Isabel kissed the jade-eyed hawk (indeed
he was pleased). And as storytellers do attest,
the hawk became a prince! May GOD be blest!

Border Crossings

in the cloudscapes of her childhood home

monarchs anointed
fragrant   meadow   asters
luminaries of heaven arose
one trillion monarchs
on Atlantic cliffs
monarch after monarch
lay larvae on undersides of milkweed leaves
chrysalis glazed jade
festooning   jasper   onyx   gold
roaming Triptychs of Camerino

but now entomologists report a 90 percent decline of migrant black
danaid butterflies   few remain   dying from herbicides
development   climate change   destruction
of fertile fields and meadows

Spaniards call them   wanderers   vagrants   nomads

each vagrant dead from glyphosate
is one less of a migrating whole   when a monarch
caterpillar feeds on leaves of milkweed   a migratory miracle
a luminary of heaven a jeweled pollinator is born praising the wind

such a hot wind last summer
in the land of the free
no monarchs
no mating in air
no glimpse of wings in seeking sanctuary

where are our wanderers in the land of the free?

Into the Desert

Like a northern pygmy-owl
on the Dungeness Spit
alone on a moonless coast
he lay awake in winter silence.
Prey to the Cooper hawk,
he took shelter in hollowed spruce
and shore debris. Days drifted white
into night after black night. He dreaded
those maudlin dawns. In desolation's
shadow he pitied those prey to peevish
stupors of psychopharmaceuticals—
temazeslam, diazedamn, clonazespam,
roads to apodictic habituation, cataclysmic
disinhibition, apocalyptic annihilation.
But wasn't he imprisoned himself?
He so wanted to be freed. He wanted
a divine intervention, and then
it came surprisingly in an owl's song—
'With-draw, with-draw-awe,
wander with me, we'll find sun.'
Hear his eschatology on detoxology—
In spring, I left for the Jemez,
the pueblo, the place of the *Padre,*
where days thunder without clouds.
I climbed Resurrection Canyon, where
water flows beneath eagle wings.
I stayed seven-times-seven-times-seventy days,
sweaty in benzene rings of withdrawal.

Shrinks call it withdrawal syndrome—
panic attacks, tremors, brain fog,
sleeplessness, dry retching…
But, I knew I was never alone.
The sound of clear crystal springs rose
from the earth, music flowing.
I rested in fragrant sage.
I rested in a hummingbird's song.
I slept as a young child again.

A Disaster of War

Distraught in shattered thought
Jonathan left Lewis-McChord
and his only friend, a peregrine, behind.
Driving over the Narrows Bridge,
the bellicose light in the sky depressed him.
The shrink said, *You need ECT—immediately.*
Jon scoffed, *I'd rather stick fucking needles in my eyes.*
        Jon imagined being sober.
He'd miss whiskey, weed, Prozac.
Before Afghanistan, before
the breakdown, he'd been happy.
        He sped the highway
in his rusted red Chevy for seven
days. Drunk out of his mind,
he pulled onto an unsigned road
in the Sonoran Badlands.
Stumbling through sagebrush,
he sat on a willowed riverbank
and closed his eyes. The *piñón* smelled
of childhood, red mesas, blue space, the rez.
        A coyote sat down to talk with him
under the shade of a cottonwood tree.
A wizened desert box turtle scolded the coyote,
Be quiet, can't you see he's going to implode?
Which is when his friend the peregrine,
whose wings were soundless in the wind, hovered
over him, and which is when Jonathan saw
the lunar blue mesa. Walking to the mesa,
he climbed a ladder into a cave and

there he stayed.
        His memories,
as if a wolf in half-light at night, hunted
him: strikes, bombs, ordnance,
the voice of commands.
Night after night he reconnoitered
the dead, war mayhem in his head.
        For you see,
he'd blown little ones to bits,
killed children, they'd done nothing
wrong, yet we left them unburied.
Jon had served, but deserved
no consolation. He prayed, but
got no answer. At last, one dawn,
Jon saw someone below and called out,
Where are you from? The man said,
Abiquiu. I've been looking for you.
Jon said, *Brother, can you keep me company?*
        And for forty days,
in an agony without words,
in a silence, a silence like a tomb,
they prayed and fasted.
And on the last day,
the sky was a sublime theophany,
a call of children from the clouds
casting shadows over the sand,
butterfly wings—blue and black
and gold. Myriads. Countless.
They were the children.
They were souls of the dead.

Elegy for the World's Neglect

For childhood poverty, death, ignorant ignorance.
For unfulfilled promises of cleanliness—
alpine meadows, mountain streams, clear skies.
And don't forget the horror of rape,
rapine ugliness, on the news, next door,
even in *Algérie*. Who cares?

Ending with an Unanswered Question

young and free
on the seaside edge
her hair a tangled rebellion
wading in water
watching her own
shadow   not on the sand
where kelp crab crawl
but in green eel grass where solar
tides collide with lunar tides
magnified by noontime sun
bioluminescence light *de anima*
man-o'-wars counterilluminate
the child bewildered
asks why the ocean
holds predators

In Another Version

she hid in lilac groves
a haven of blooms
above the *bohereen*
playing maiden fair
laying an altar of dandelions

a nymph
calmed at the sea edge
sea morse ~ sea spray ~ sea hags
sea blue-grey ~ sea yarns ~ sea walls ~ sea wrack

there she was free (for a while) from the panting boy never dear to her, her mother's sister's pockmarked son who stunk of skunk and stale beer, a maggot who ate her soul. neighbors gossiped. as if she didn't know. why does she run away, walk the cliffs alone regardless of the weather. as if they really cared? really. *Jesus, Mary, and Joseph*, where in God's name is her mother?

banshees shriek inside her head
you're a dirty shit

only six years old, more or less, so we're told
she drowns in stormy nightmares
melancholy and sad at heart
the world was more full of weeping than she could u^{n}*derstand*
plagued by Satan   Prince of Darkness   goblins
they played treachery
she hid in books
fairies called aerially
come away to waters wild

she hoped for happiness, moving to the world of old ways, to *Sceilig Mhór* where rain keens, herbs grow wild, learning the language of birds, secret love-talkers. there a monk taught her to read her dreams

Dreams are a minaret of the soul

she dreamt under open skies
she dreamt things true
she dreamt herself into being

now / she understands / she is not / a metaphor / for a paedophilia

Concerning Light Inside of Darkness

There was a young man who was deeply troubled.
Trapped in a hornet's nest of anxiety, stung by years
of war, he asked the Lord, 'Can you forgive me?'
He understood he'd committed many a sin.

Each night, drenched in sweat, his dreams were
a bottomless abyss: demons, masters of deceit
haunted him. Each day, he would walk about
sad and distressed. Day nor night took pity.

Struggling, he sought out psychiatrists and the banalities
of therapies: EMDR, CBT, DBT, ECT. Hoping to live
normally, he tried Zerzone, Zoloft, Prozac, Ativan,
Ketamine, Klonopin, Remeron, but got no better.

One August an old Jesuit told him, 'Nightmares,
themes in dreams, are your best friend.' There was no
better priest, for you see, Father Paul prayed earnestly,
praised God, and understood the trauma of war.

'Friend,' he said, 'make a journey with me through
your clouded canvas of dreams to be freed from fiends
embedded in your head.' The priest, an everyday
mystic, was well known for his gift of discernment.

On retreat, the young man had nightmares—
sniper attacks, mass casualties, airstrikes. At night
he dreamt of a mother, father, and two young sons
killed by his M67 fragmentation grenades.

In distress from his unrest, the young man
confessed in a gnawing anxiety, 'Father Paul,
No one deserves to die like that, whole families
blameless. I'm sickened by the foulness of my sin.'

Like Virgil guiding Dante, the old Jesuit helped
the young man find light in darkness. Paul said,
'Invite Jesus into your dreams, imagine a peaceful
place, perhaps with a lover.' He dreamt foreign

voices, he dreamt a thousand ravens pecking
at the family's wounds, feeding on the slaughter—
blood pouring onto foreign plains. Once again
he confessed, 'Father, war was never dear to me,

but love, that I can understand.' The young man
never banished embattled grief from his daily life.

What followed, I can't say. That part of the story
remains untold. Móna is the name of the versifier
who wrote this poem while in exile. She gives
thanks for the old Jesuit. Amen

Where Does One Begin

Port Townsend, WA

James, a poet versed in Yeats and Joyce,
a lover of Juvencus's *Walking on Water*,
had a fire-soul daughter. He damascened
her soul with fiery-gold—she inherited
the family gift of poetry. But James died
at an early age, snatching her happiness away,
vanishing with the moon. Walking a path
upon the sea, Mudnahait drowned in raging
waves and a turbulent storm of sorrow.

What happened to her fire-soul?
Ah, the strangest things. Though she was born
to see with her heart, her only certainty
was impermanence. She became deranged.
Some called it 'an imagined self.' She coined
it misdiagnoses masquerading as physician
discomfort (in high vogue): cognitive
dysmorphic dysfunction, neurotransmitter
malfunction, emotional defunction.

Why prescribe soporifics bound
by interaction hell? Moody Amitriptyline,
carte blanche Fluoxetine, calm green Gabitril,
hypnotic rose Ambien? Caution advised,
black box warnings: sleep-driving, confusion,
delusion, loss of memory, not knowing

you're having sex, feeling sad or empty.
She dreams of getting out of herself,
an emergence as someone new, a balanchine
butterfly borne on a breeze.

June illumines milk-blue windows in Star
of the Sea. She goes to the confessional:
'My life's rife with anger *ad nauseam*, a crater
of sadness, like a small infant left alone,
or a victim of war.' 'Why don't you write?
Find a poet's tongue? Place yourself in God's
hand, become a child again? You need
to retreat.' She drove home in the dark.

IV

On the Brink of the Sea

El Retiro San Iñigo, Los Altos California

Muadnait rose early in the *morning*
to drink black tea and pray a *prayer* –
LORD I implore illumine my *children*.
She made a journey to the brink of the *sea*
where she saw a chapel upon a hill of *grass*
whose windows were ablaze with *light*

reflecting the singing sea's golden *light*.
A song of a hermit thrush filled the *morning*
as swallows swooned over marsh *grass*,
sweet melodists of the wind. Hear my *prayer*
LORD, protect them. The sea roared love, the *sea*
sang sestines. She wondered why her *children*

lived amongst thorn and thistle. Her *children*
had once played all manner of pranks in *delight*
on the beach on the shore by the bright blue *sea*
so long ago. She dwelt on fear that very *morning*,
and asked, 'Is life inane insanity or most holy *prayer*?'
She climbed the hill of fresh mown *grass*

on stairs of stone woven in worn green *grass*
to the chapel of Monserrat. There, *children*
of God cross to the other side in eremite *prayer*.
There, Muadnait stayed and fasted in anchorite *light*
for one year and a day, dreaming dreams of *mourning*
doves cooing songs of praise to the pristine *sea*.

At night gloom stormed those dreams with *sea*
fevers as demons danced on fire scorched *grass.*
That May, a dragonfly woke her one *morning,*
calling her by name—'Muadnait, your *children*
are mending. Tonight, pray in moon *light.*'
Confused, she complained, 'But, *prayer*

in darkness is all I know.' He hummed, '*Prayer*—
your plea—is a rueful leaf falling to a peaceful *sea.*'
Astounded by the crazy dragonfly in *flight,*
she sought out the holy man on the hill of *grass.*
He was afire, caught up in a trance—'Your *children*
are a small unfolding of *morning.*'

Prayer is wind's praise through bent green *grass.*
Prayer is a sapphire *sea* brooding. Prayer is *children*
in womblike rubel*lite* aborning a jadeite *morning.*

Song Weaver

Not every day but most days I spend
in turmoil of mind, yet you welcomed
me a stranger from the west, saying
'Come rest in your father's mother's mother's
heel stone cottage on the bluff by the sea.'
Together we washed weir wood floors with wild hyssop;
scrubbing mud walls with euphrasy and rue;
cleansing typhus windows with rosemary and lavender;
brewing bee balm tea in that calm place.
You carried a book of poems and brought
a bottle of *Chave Hermitage* to the lilac grove
where dunnocks weave nests in hedgerows.
I opened my mind to you, and you opened
my heart to me. I leaned in and you opened
to the page where we'd left off:
'You can bend the woods with blossom,
what is there you cannot do?
God, I ask for two things only,
heaven when my life is done,
payment as befits a poem—a son.'
Our friendship, priceless,
altered everything I do.

My Confessor

Franciscan Friary, Cork, Ireland

Amidst embittered trouble, war broke
out. Crossing the portico, seeking
sanctuary, we wait in quietude.
Or in turpitude?

I enter the confessional.
He loved that I was American.
I was taken by his brown robe.
And from its fold he pulled out
The Unbearable Lightness of Being, and
in his poet voice read aloud to me,
'A person who longs to leave the place
where she lives is an unhappy person.'
We talked for an hour.

Was I being made anew?

He went on to recite
his own poetry
from memory—

They say love doesn't' change,
but deepens, becomes ever new,
alters shade, like the Kerry Sea
in the bay, beside which we grew
and matured as good wine.

We talked for an hour.
Peaceful stillness compassed
everything in his presence.
GLORY BE TO GOD,
I soared out that door.
And as if in ecstasy,
walking marble floors, I passed
tightlipped penitents, who muttered,
'Jesus, Mary, and Joseph,
LORD bless us and save us,
what in God's name did she do?'

Sea Muse

I am awake in my dream a wild waif
weaving words written on wind

I am a golden eagle   no seamew perched
on a lofty rock above the sound spearing
fish in misted winter waters

I am a killdeer nesting near cold water
in March on green grass
I feign brokenness   my brood grows

I am a vesper thrush clearing
my mind like a monk composing
sin and songs of love

I am a red-tailed hawk hovering high
in the sky-haunting trees with no names
from the summit of a steep silent cliff

I am a western meadowlark lingering
beneath a branch by a boisterous brook
a flute-player of folk ballads

I am a marsh wren dancing a waltz
on swaying cattails by the seashore
meandering   wondering   merrying

I am a goldfinch on a glorious May morn
filching thistle under the shadow of a cedar
my flock flies freely

I am a violet-green swallow skimming
the glimmering pond on a gay August
evening where the sun never sets

I am a dove clothed in a cloak of holiness
taking wing to my dovecote by the cove
I envy no one

Our Lady of the Pines

Plodding through pines to the *place*
Paul had said to go I felt hopelessly *blue*
and doubted this pilgrim way, but I *still*
continued on. Hadn't Paul said, 'Remember *love*
sees light and flies while the dawn is still *dark*'?
And while ambling along under August's *sun*,

I watched a damselfly catch the *sun*.
Tired, I laid on the forest floor, a womblike *place*,
and began to pray. A nearby meadow*lark*
played a pitch-perfect flute, sounding 'Who are *you*?'
A wind rained needles of pine from *above*.
Couchant, I stayed *still*.

Hadn't Paul said, 'Be perfectly *still*'?
And then under a rising *sun*,
a hermit thrush sang a hymnody of *love,*
echoing throughout the trees in that *place*
of peace. I heard lightening wings as a hawk *flew*
forcefully, and the crow's *stark*

'Khaaaa' marked death. Was it *dark*
desolation in flight? *Still*
couchant I *knew,*
I'd confused love with hate. The *sun*
illumed my childhood defilement in *disgrace*.
Then one thousand skylarks soared *above*,

as I wondered, 'What is *love*?'
Pine boughs swayed as the meadow*lark*
sang woodnotes in that green pine *place.*
All grew still, splendidly *still,*
under the sun, a vibrant *sun*,
when a vision in mystical *blue*,

in lapis lazuli *blue*,
debouched in rays of sun *above*.
And under autumnal *sun*,
the wind whispered a *Petrarch*
sestine of love 'Be *still*
in the poetry of *place*.'

I awoke to *love* in hues of *blue*
in *still* solitude, in that *place*
a *dark* abyss fled from the *Son*.

Litany of Birde

I am a star on obsidian seas
I am a wind sounding solitude
I am a hawk above the cliffs
I am a storm beyond wild oceans
I am a sea-queen of poet's dreams

I am a doe of the forest green
I am an alder embracing wind
I am a white flowering wood
I am a thorn-tree before the door
I am a home for travelers worn

I am a blackbird of festal mirth
I am a dragonfly stitching verse
I am a thrush amongst the rushes
I am a hummingbird courting love
Many poems are in my wings

I am a rain replenishing fields
I am a stream flowing estuarine
I am the dew anointing green grass
I am a brook singing prosody
We speak of verse

I am an aster amongst brambles
I am the moon in virgin white

I am snow falling apatite
I cover a multitude of sin
Where shall we begin?

I am dawn breathing in your garden
I am a rose closed and unadorned
I am a portico to be blest
I am your rose bloomed incarnadine
Beloved, come to me.

Cento: Fourth Chapter on Love

I

Remember catching fire
on our way to love,
to the song of birds
taking flight in harbour
light? Remember catching
fire listening to the song
weaver's sorrow, yearning
for the heartbeat of God?

But then you left—
Left me on the other side
of longing in a silent land
where women sing by the wind
and the sea and midnight tides.
And there, poets of anti-poems
and early Christian poets rejoice
in the gospel. And there, recusant
poets are secret keepers,
who by word of mouth sigh
news of poetry's promise:
Unless you become like a child,
like children of Húrin, the other wind,
the shadow roads, the house of chains,
with a gathering of gargoyles,
will be a storm of swords.

II

And then, after a night
with my confessor,
Saint Ignatius of Loyola,
the mystic of everyday life—
I walked into the sea.
Then and there, in the fullness
of faith, I cried like a bell.

Later in a room of my own,
I had a conversation with Denise
Levertov. But Denise spoke
in broken Latin, reading
Novum Testamentum Graece Et Latine—
arguing the new evangelization
and the need of prayer, and
I didn't understand.

III

Returning home, I watched
light on winged birds
of Puget Sound, foraged
healing herbs, walked
Crystal Springs, out of the path
of darkness into heaven's
wind, into a cloud of unknowing.

Can't you see?
You're the eldest, fearing—
'She loves me not,

my inheritance has fallen.'
I'm a foundling, bearing—
a girl who played with fire,
a girl who kicks the hornets' nest.
I'm a divergent fire of love.

IV

Remember our pilgrimage—
Loyola, San Sebastián, Monserrat?
Making love on mossflowers
under a Joshua tree? When there
was no moon we shared
tales of the Alhambra.

And I matured in the landscape
of love, battling demons of darkness,
battling the dark angel who'd brought
nightmares of terror into my life.
For Sabriel, the fire bringer,
brought dreamsongs, and
once again, we caught fire
on the way to love.

Paradise

Camaldoli Hermitage, Big Sur, CA

I found a place that knows not time.
At the end of the sea, an indigo mystery,
where infinity speaks to skies of mauve,
rose, blue, to the sun whose warmth
dispels March's gray, green, brown.

A bell calls, one lone bell of the hermitage.
We weave baskets of praise and petition,
woven like dunnocks' nests of twigs,
moss, and wool—songs etched in filigreed
smoke of myrrh—hearts afire.

My cell. One bed. One table.
One cross. One door to the garden.
Dianthus, thyme, droning honeybees—
stir memories of barefoot wonder.
On the wall hangs one rule of Romuald—

Sit in your cell as in paradise.
Put the whole world behind you and forget it.
Watch your thoughts like a good
fisherman watching for fish.
The path you must follow
is in the Psalms—never leave it.

The moon offers light—
washing stucco walls white,
as stars in counterpoint ignite,
and one nightjar *churrs*
rest in my wine-dark night.

Cento: Landscape of the Soul

I

I'm a peasant girl who hums
praise, gathering wild herbs—
fennel, marjoram, thyme,
wishing to be free from hate.
Enwombed within white-washed
walls, I kneel
in a faraway place that
knows secrets of the rising
sun, writing my name on the sand,
tilling the soil by hand, lining
furrows full of dark-sown
seed serene.

Hours pass like clouds—
sweet melodies drifting
through the garden as a devoted
dove coos sacred harmony.
Like scents borne on a breeze,
a poem catches white cherry petals,
fluttering down like snow without
a poet's conceit.

In the blue May sky,
when spring is purple,
and the warmth of love
has brought the rose to bloom,

I watch a stork teach
her fledglings how to make
use of their wings.

II

Lending an ear to the winds tale,
I amble barefoot on pilgrimage
across a field, a desirable place
for one who is tired—
hyacinth, angel flower, bee's flower,
affirm the wind's alchemy.
Algarrobo trees refresh me from
noon-time sun. The orchard
faces the sea's blues
with all its greens, and
I sleep peacefully
in cool shade—
then dream.

I dream of happiness
snatched away, vanished
like noon dew, a memory,
a moment of inscribed
impermanence.

Walking a path
to the sea, remembering
the moon loved me, and he,
the holder of my heart followed

me, waves echoing verse borne
on malachite seas.

Love, what would you
have had me say? Hold me
here forever beside the sea?
In the secret dip of solitary
dunes on hot secluded sands,
lay your body in my arms,
take me? Come live with me
and be my love forever?

III

Now nightfalls, falling as night falls,
someone calls. I don't know how
to answer. The shape of a song
on my tongue creates what can't
be seen. A strophe of a poem?

In the home of a poet
beside the sea, there's always
a lament of youth and love
with swiftness of wind
whose verse is sung
everywhere at the turn
of a wing. In the home
of a good poet the scent
of the sea awakens poetry.

V

Barefoot Abandon

To burn with desire and keep quiet about it is the greatest punishment we can bring on ourselves. ~FEDERICO GARCÍA LORCA

Last night we were free   the moon   you   me.
Our lips of spiced cinnabar burned through the dark
and in barefoot abandon   we dove into the sea.

You   an azurite combustion   me   the Rose of Tralee.
We swam clear coastal waters with a great white shark.
Last night we were free   the moon   you   me.

An offshore breeze seduced us so innocently.
We shed shift and shirt and ran to the seamark
and in barefoot abandon we dove into the sea.

and rose so breathless I would not foresee
so fickle a kiss. Why leave me in the dark?
Last night we were free   the moon   you   me

for my heart and love are eternal you see.
You singed my lips   burned your watermark,
when in barefoot abandon   we   dove into the sea.

You haunt my dreams with wild anxiety
I yearn for the years I lost you   my Irish anarch.
Last night we were free   the moon   you   me.
Barefoot   abandoned   I dove into the sea.

Townies

We are the dreamers of dreams wandering lone sea-breakers.
~ ARTHUR O'SHAUGHNESSY

We trespassed Osher Ledge in October when gale winds empty summer estates of Blue-Blood-Brahmins. The road was ours alone. We broke into a shuttered home not our own, finding faded letters stained with tears and beeswax and wine. Leaning close, our love caught fire—ocean madness—a feverish sea-fever afresh and ablaze. And when we returned to towne all-a-tremble passing bowing reeds and two mute swans, you stole one kiss from me. But now you're dead and I'm lost in dreams wandering a sea-wracked sea-strand scrivened in innocence. How sad our words were left unsaid?

Don't You Know

Cohasset's a town on the edge of the murmuring
coast, where most folk are wealthy, boasting
blue-blood lineage, and clubbish, published pedigrees.
A good man from the next town called Scituate,

James the carpenter, was much sought after for his skill.
One December day, gale winds roared from the east,
blowing off the roof of an arrogant hedge-fund manager
who was too well shaved, wordy, and silver tongued.

He insisted James come post haste (taking careless
pleasure in bullish snobbery). No shirker, James drove
north to the guy's ostentatious estate on Jerusalem Road.
A fierce Atlantic gust blew James off the scaffolding!

Falling forty feet, he broke arms, legs, feet, and a clavicle
to boot. Truth to tell, he awoke eleven weeks later from a drug-induced
coma. Crippling pain tortured his body like *Tomás*
de Torquemada's rack. Despite gobbling opioids, benzos,

edibles, and cheap red wine, his pain remained—that fact
is he all but went insane. Blottoed, annihilated, he passed
out every day. He lost his salt-box house, Dodge Ram;
he even lost his lovely wife. He bamboozled townies

and hoodwinked friends. In time, they felt no pity—
they deemed him dead. Homeless, crack-brained,

he mainlined smack and became a stealthful thief.
Although James loved his mother with all his heart,

he did the vilest thing—he stole her wedding ring.
Ashamed, filled with self-loathing, James sought
out the monk from Our Lady of Glastonbury Abbey,
who'd baptized, married, and buried his dad.

As luck would have it the monk was there. 'Father,
I'm wicked fucked up, am I going to hell? I tried
to clean up using Buprenorphine, Dolophine,
Naltrexone, even state rehab. For God's sake,

I even stole my mum's Claddagh wedding ring.'
In that ostensibly off-the-wall, devil-may-care way
of old age, the monk said, 'My nephew was hooked
on crack and drank too—ending up in jail twice.

We packed him off to Mombasa where
a Maryknoller works with orphans,
refugees, HIV whores, and more.
He performed a miracle on my sister's son.'

That very day, the monk asked a wealthy man
(who gave alms to atone for many a past egregious sin)
to pay for the carpenter's flight—which he did!
Mombasa was green in humidity, in which

poverty strained—the like you've never seen.
The labyrinthed alleys were as winding as an Irish

fairytale. The first forty days he wretched, sweated,
waited for that miracle, waited for the end of the war.

He wanted to be reborn. I don't know when,
but one dawn he opened his eyes with a fogged
sense that he was awakening into a dream.
Could his goodness, which had shown no sign

of itself over the past ten years, reappear?
Outside he could hear children playing, sounding
exactly like they did back then—he could have sworn—
when he'd play games with his sister Mona

on a summer morn. Was he going crazy?
He got up, slowly drawing aside the tattered
shade. The sight of the playing children
(in the Maryknoller's care) moved him.

The truth is—in the end—he stayed.
Namshukuru Mungu.

Loneliness

A woman's not a poet, but a poem. ~ SEÁN PÁDRAIG Ó RÍORDÁIN

She sought solitude,
not loneliness,
to understand,
not self-loath,
to live in a saltbox
home by the shore,
and at night burn
bayberry candles, and drink
Bordeaux or a Guinness (or two)
with her lovers three
(Amergin, Hartnett, O'Shaughnessy),
and write, as an owl in flight,
poems of lust and druery.
Will she join the madding crowd?
Mingle loneliness with other's happiness?
Crawl into the bed with lecherous men?
Or better yet, pick up the pen?

Albariño

A goldfinch on the highest branch burns with brilliance, as if offering all its joy to us, as if its song, night-into-dawn, cries, 'The beauty of it all.' August alights in warm fullness, Cascades and Olympics arch a purple backwash into infinity, and the sky's arrayed with violet-green swallows swooning and rubied hummingbirds courting as a full-moon blesses Mount Rainer. We chime glass after glass after glass of *Albariño*. Ah, evening. We talk as blossoms fall from roses divine. I say, 'I'm leaving you.' We quarrel without a kiss. And there, outside the window, screech owls trill, trill, trill, their melodies clamoring for love.

February

The sun's still low and
Indian plum blooms a bit
of fragrance. Across the pond
a heron contemplates the bdellium-gray
bay. And in the moonlit
morning all lies still—
brambles and branches,
buoys and boats,
even cat-o'-nine-tails,
until a sharp-shinned hawk
pierced a shaft of light.
The scattered piles of twigs
erupted uneasily in blackbird trills.
And when the deadening
north wind crossed
the marsh, ferrying
memories, she asked
herself the question
echoed by the wind.
How long can grief go on?
She missed her husband's
caress. Wrapped in wool,
she watched an eagle soar,
her thoughts following
his turbulent flight.

March

Leaving the island's cold stone shore behind, I ferry the Wenatchee to Colman Dock, walk from the ferry to the train, ride the train to the transcontinental plane, then land near the Gulf of Mexico. And on the beach, an osprey child, a hatchling the size of one's heart, cries for its father—incessantly. The shore calls and shells answer—whelk, scallop, shards of conk—as if childhood melodies. And as if a child, I swim with manatees—but the taste of salt recalls a loss unconsoled. One month before my father died he wrote: *If I could only walk into the abode of purity, the wild sea undefiled, I'd finish this poem for you my child.* And here on the warm shore I'm consoled by cadences of the sea.

Poets' Daughters

Each day Haydn prayed prior to composing.
Cloistered in study walls imaged in tourmaline, ochre,
verdigris, I pray under Venetian Veneziano's
Madonna and Child—framed in gold.

Most days my maple desk is all but bare,
an altar adorned with a shamrock vase from Galway,
and a bookmark of *San Juan,* Patron of Writers painted in
Taos—both from my daughter.

Most days I pray the bookmark's pyrographed words,
'Writer of gospel and epistles, your writing brought
benefit to the world, I humbly ask
that my writing might bring benefit too.'

My poet father watches over me, fountainpen in hand,
from a monochrome photo sixty-five-years old—
framed in black. I'm told I was one when he passed.

My window overlooks a marsh,
where a white sage moon overlooks the sea,
winter light catching a finch filching
milkweed seed, singing consort with the wind.

And the rose garden, as if dead, lies still,
swaddled by a willowed fence I wattled last summer
while kneeling in June perfume. And in its midst,
shovel in hand stands *San Fiarce*, Patron of Gardeners.

Most days I wonder why my father stays so present in his absence.
    And in my cell, my fountainpen tills birth and death,
        and on my altar a postcard sits, a white cross
        atop an adobe wall against an endless sky.

And on that postcard of New Mexico's cloudless sky,
    my daughter wrote: 'Mum, when we're brave
    enough to face darkness, we'll find light.'

Poet's Son

ocotillo pierce
a bit of the sky
over the hill
the path falls
into stillness
under a noonday sun
all lies still—tranquil & still
even the squamata
chuckwalla & inquana
all but a withering wind
we walk the trail
mother and son
my son speaks of poetry
consonance   caesura   enjambment
overhead the fire burns
blindingly blue
I'm old
I stumble & fall
then
under the shade
of an acacia tree
he recites *Zelaya* from memory

I wish that you would never take my mother,
for I should wish to tend her as a child
and put her to sleep with kisses,
when somewhat old,
as she may need the sun.

his words hold me

Andalusian Way

My friend the Jesuit said, 'Write a love poem.'
I thought, why not, then took a plane to Spain,
to *Almería*. Barefoot in seafoam,
in sea blue-greens, I fell in love again,
for there on *Mojácar's* warm windswept beach,
Juan Ramón Jiménez arose from the sea.
Under the moonscape we caught fire, each
embrace, each feverish touch inflamed me
in that land of dark *Monastrell* and musk.
Clasped in pleasure we collapsed into bed
of a thousand yearning kisses at dusk.
Upon my return the Jesuit said,
'Did you write that love poem, a Song of Songs?'
'Father, I must confess, not until dawn.'

I Give Myself Up

Our love's a willow bough of pleasure
swaying all night with the wind
in tumultuous fierce desire.
Our love's a willow bough of pleasure—
your provocative kiss, you clever
rogue, taking me so quick to sin.
Our love's a willow bough of pleasure
        swaying all night.

Ancient Quarrel

My mother heard from her mother,
who'd heard from her mother's mother,
who heard from our ancient clan north
of Galway Bay, that Moná,
Irish for *little noble one*,
meant I was to be an ode
of Irish nobility. She'd
wanted a son!

Over the Rockies,
heavy with sage and monarchs,
a monastery looks west where
whales breach. And there, in Pacific
light, a white-robed monk spoke eloquently.
And when I begged, 'Father help me,'
his hands in his lap held a stillness
new to me. 'Mona? Latin origin means
solitude, alone, solitary. It's unclear to me
why you're such a storm of crashing seas?
Perhaps you're an onomatopoeic verse?'

Below Tesuque Pueblo
lies Santa Fe in cloudless wonder
where sage wafts. I met a woman there,
on the mesa—an I'raquian exile.
'You have a beautiful name in Fársí ىَنُم,'
she laughed, it means—
desire, wanting, unreachable prayer.'
Am I a pun?

Except that, those months in Mombasa,
on coastal shores, working with HIV whores
(who were old enough to be my mother),
I was not a prayer. The whores laughed
too, for they knew me as *mona guenon*
the *white long-tailed monkey* (named by the Moors),
and it was close to being true—those monkeys
thrashing through banana trees with me.
Am I a mixed-metaphor?

Médecins Sans Frontières missioned
me to Abkhazia, as if I were a spook,
to study death. I couldn't bear the cold.
Each breath frosted folktales on the looking glass.
At night, we drowned December's misery
in *D'Usse Cognac*, glass after glass after glass. Drunk,
the Triestine physician laughed and asked,
'What was your mother thinking?
In our native tongue your name means—
cunt, pussy, crazy one, but generally *an idiot*.'
What kind of mother tongue is that?

At last I made it to Spain,
Mojácar to be exact, to write poetry,
as if the sound of mating owls in the dark of night
would muse me. Instead, well as a matter of fact,
my name, meaning *drunkenness* in *el Española*,
amused the locals in the shops. All I know—
it made them laugh, and for a time,

I found happiness in *Monastrell's* ruby-hue,
dreaming nude poems in the arms of another.
Is this Lorca's *duende*?

All this left me wondering
about my mother and my name.
She'd nicknamed me the village *idiot*,
because it's sort of true. I live a *solitary*
life in light-hearted *drunkenness*,
leaping like a grinning *guenon* in thrashing
memories. But, I'm not sure why
my brother calls me *cunt*. Are you?
Doesn't matter anyway, as I told him
'Fuck you.' Not so *noble* words,
but ancient quarrels heat the heart.
Tell me, friend, will I weep when
he's laid in our seaside cemetery?

Moná. A triple-entendre?

Sacred Moment

The Pacific's clear and green as celadon,
and, although summer, it feels like fall.
August winds blow steadily from the north,
and the pungent scent of dying kelp wafts
a sadness.   Snow plovers,
sanderlings, osprey soar sovereign overhead
as I walk the turning tides. Killdeers skirt
the tideline. A gull stands still as obsidian:
not scavenging, not stealing, not colonizing.
Barefoot, bundled,   baffled
(for being a fisherman's daughter, I know
it should take flight), I thought how odd.
And when I saw the fishing line, nearly invisible,
wound round the gull—it's wings bleeding,
feet entangled like a snare—I cast my coat
as if a net, catching the gull, swaddling
it to my breast, calming it as if my child,
heart on heart, kneeling in the dunes, until
a handsome stranger came along. Without
thinking, without speaking, only hoping
its wings would fly, and that it wouldn't die,
he and I cut the line, undoing the knots,
removing the barbed hook. And when
it took flight, an audience of seven young
children applauded in awe and delight.
And then,   I thought about you.
I thought about the wounds of marriage.
I thought about the obscurities of love.
And then I thought   about me.

And so I made my way to the monastery
on the cliffs of Big Sur, in search of peace.
And I found brother Isaiah in prayer
and asked him his   thoughts.
Thoughts on entanglement. And after
a night of prayer, Isaiah the monk said
to me, 'You ought to hold your spouse,
heart to heart, wound to wound, and
hope to hope.'

Notes

Cento: Laudato Si'

The poem patches together poetry and writings of Wendell Berry, Pope Francis, Seán Pádraig Ó Ríordáin, Rainer Maria Rilke, Michael Longley, Jeanie Thompson, Anita Endrezze, John Montague, Ernesto Mejía Sánchez, St. Francis of Assisi, John of the Cross, Jorge Carrera Andrade, Dante, Michael Hartnett, Patriarch Bartholomew, Mona Lydon-Rochelle, Benedict XVI, Amergin, and Alfonso Guillén Zelaya.

Sand Hills

Na hÉireannaigh means 'the Irish.'

Nora's Child

Farm colony was the official term for Grafton State Hospital for chronically insane patients that Massachusetts operated from 1901 to 1973. The Hassanamisco are a group of Nipmuc Indians native to Grafton, Massachusetts. Thelonious Monk, the famous jazz pianist, was admitted to Grafton in 1957.

Miraculous Water Birth of Jésus

Alice Gautreau, a Médecins Sans Frontières midwife, reports the story as told to her by the Cameroonian woman who gave birth prior to being rescued by the Aquarius in the Central Mediterranean on July 11, 2017.

Adonai and the Mai Aini Refugee Camp, 2017

Mai Aini refugee camp in northern Ethiopia is home to more than 18,000 refugees from neighboring Eritrea. Jesuit Refugee Service provides services and activities to help residents deal with the trauma of their flight to safety and camp life.

In Another Version

Verses are from W.B. Yeats, *Irish Myth, Legend, and Folklore,* and Anita Endrezze, *Throwing Fire at the Sun, Water at the Moon.*

Poet's Son

The verse is from Alfonso Zelaya's poem "Lord, I ask a Garden."

My Confessor

The Unbearable Lightness of Being, Milan Kundera (Faber and Faber, London, 1985). The verse "*They say love does not change...*" is from Iain Duggan's *The Song Weaver,* Ariel Press, Ireland, 2011.

Song Weaver

The verse is from Giolla Brighde MacNamee's late thirteenth-century poem, "Childless," as translated by Frank O'Connor.

Cento: Fourth Chapter on Love

Comprised of book titles from the poet's home by the following authors: Karl Rahner, Anthony de Mello, Derek Mahon, Paul Lynch, Tana French, Stieg Larrson, Virginia Woolf, Tomáš Halík, Harvey D. Egan, Hans Urs von Balthasar, Madeline L'Engle, Denise Levertov, Nicanor Parra, Louise Imogen Guiney, OP, Kate Morton, William Carlos Williams, Philip Levine, J.R.R. Tolkien, Ursula K. Le Guin, Sean Russell, Meredith Pierce, George Martin, Robert Frost, Christopher Paolini, Lloyd Alexander, Paulo Coehlho, Evagrius Ponticus, Brian Jacques, U2, Dag Hammarskjold, Washington Irving, Moira Linehan, Piers Anthony, Ronan Bennett.

Cento: Landscape of the Soul

Comprised of verse taken from Marilyn Nelson, Saint Patrick, John of the Cross, Faltonia Betitia Proba, Alfonso Guillén Zelaya,

Gonzalo de Berceo, Rafael Alberti, Dante, Ernesto Mejía Sánchez, Juvencus, Antonio Machado, Paulinus of Nola, Jorge Carrera Andrade, Christopher Marlowe, and Song of Songs.

Don't You Know

Namshukuru Mungu means *Thanks be to God* in Kiswahili.

Made in the USA
Columbia, SC
31 January 2020

87243632R00076